TABLE OF CONTENT

MW00603928

CHAPTER I

GETTING STARTED

ORGANIZING YOUR JOB SEARCH

If you are looking for a job now, according to current statistics, you will be looking for a job again within the next three to five years. There are good jobs out there, but the reality in today's world is that it requires hard work and ingenuity to get them.

It is helpful to look at the job search process as a unique opportunity to learn the techniques that will help you gain control over your career and continue to manage it well. These include:

- Identifying your skills and defining a career objective.
- Writing a resume that will survive a 30-second scan.
- Researching the market and developing a search strategy.
- Networking and utilizing contacts productively.
- Mastering interviewing techniques.

Above all, *preparation, practice* and a *positive mental outlook* are the keys to a successful job search.

Rarely do individuals go through a major career change alone. Almost all of us need a "partner" or "partners" to share our thoughts, explore alternatives, and seek advice. There are three key resources to your support system.

- **Trusted Friends or Relatives.** Seek out the help of one or two of your most trusted friends. These are individuals who will support you through thick and thin. They totally believe in you and care about you. They will give you honest feedback, but in a supportive way.

- **Other Job Seekers.** You may want to get in touch with someone you know who is going through the search process. It can be helpful to share experiences and accomplishments; but more importantly, you can encourage one another, discuss strategies and exchange networking techniques.

- **Yourself.** You must be your best supporter. Believing in yourself begins with an understanding of your own strengths, abilities and interests.

TO BEGIN YOUR SEARCH:

- **List your contacts**. These should include:

    > Friends and family members
    > Current and prior business associates and acquaintances
    > Doctors, lawyers, accountants, and religious leaders
    > Acquaintances from sports, volunteer activities and professional associations

- **List three to five business references that prospective employers may call.** Be sure to contact these people and ask if they would be willing to allow you to use them as references. Later on be sure to notify them if you know that a particular person or company will be calling. (And don't forget to inform the people who have given references once you have started a new job.)

- **Begin the daily discipline of reading newspapers, trade and business publications.** Job leads can take many forms: advertisements, management promotions, company stories — opportunities take digging and study, not scanning.

- **Familiarize yourself with on-line job search services.** There is a comprehensive list of fashion and career web sites on page 59.

- **Search the Internet.** Use search engines to research a company or brand. Go to individual company web sites for information about the company, its divisions and products. Many large companies also have career sections on their sites that include listings of open positions and job descriptions.

- **Start recording expenses.** These may be tax deductible. Ask for and keep receipts when possible. Check with your tax accountant or the IRS for advice.

- **Get into the daily habit of recording and planning actions you will take**. These include meetings, contacts, references, telephone calls, letters, etc.

Your job search is hard work. It requires your *maximum commitment*, consistently and continuously. As in business, there are good days and bad days, high spots and low spots. It is important not to dwell on the low spots. Develop a mindset to take positive action when this occurs — make telephone calls, write letters, do on-line research, go to the library, review newspapers and make some cold calls. Action will help shift gears toward the positive.

Here are some common traps to avoid:

- Do not stew over the factors that have caused you to leave your last job. Leave any negativity behind you. It can only hinder your performance in getting a job. Begin looking to the future now. A positive outlook is your best asset.

- *Do not immediately* contact your personal and business associates *about a job*. You will certainly want to use these contacts, but not before you are emotionally ready and intellectually prepared to make the best use of them.

- Do not rush to contact executive recruiters. Again, there is a time for this and a particular way to initiate these contacts.

> **Do not make your search effort a part-time affair. Finding a job is a full-time job and hard work! There is a direct correlation between effort expended and level of success**

MANAGING YOUR JOB SEARCH

The management and organizational skills that you have developed during your career can be put to good use during your job search. Networking, scheduling appointments, following up with letters, researching companies and preparing for interviews requires an organized, systematic approach.

Here are a few ideas to keep in mind as you organize your job search.

- Use a portable planner or PDA to record appointments.

- Carry copies of your resume, envelopes, stamps and pens with you so that you are always prepared to respond quickly.

- Whether you use an answering machine or a voicemail service be sure your message is a brief, professional one.

- Set up a separate e-mail address for your job search. If possible, be sure it includes at least part of your name. Do not use numbers in your e-mail address. They often trigger Spam filters which automatically block the receipt of your e-mail.

- Establish a weekly planning guide to outline what is to be accomplished daily.

- Spend business hours on the contact process.

- Use off hours for research and record keeping.

The final three pages of this section contain sample forms to help you manage your job search:

- A weekly activity plan
- An interview and networking log
- A job search expense sheet

ACTIVITY PLAN

WEEK OF _____

DONE (✓)		Contact Meetings Scheduled	Phone Calls Made/ E-mails Sent	Ads & Internet Job Listings Responded To	Recruiters Contacted	Target Companies Contacted	Job Interviews Scheduled
	Monday						
	Tuesday						
	Wednesday						
	Thursday						
	Friday						
	Weekend						
	Next Week						

EXPENSE SHEET

Date	Purpose	Trains/ Cabs	Rental Cars	Auto Mileage	Parking/ Tolls	Hotel	Food	Other

CONTACTS LOG

Date	Name Title	Address Telephone	Activity Date of Contact, results, referrals, follow-up, thank-you letters

CHAPTER II

SELF-EVALUATION

Identifying your skills is the first step in writing or updating your resume. It will also help you focus your job search. Start by thinking about yourself objectively — as a product you want to market. You will need to thoroughly understand your product as well as the market that you are targeting.

In Chapter III we will discuss how to quantify your accomplishments and incorporate these skills into your resume. For the moment though, we will focus on verbalizing the ways you have used these skills. When you are interviewing, you will need to demonstrate that you have the skills that you claim to have. Think of *specific examples* of ways you utilized a particular skill and what you achieved in doing so. You may want to refer to the Action Verb List at the end of this chapter to remind you of some of your skills. The examples you select do not necessarily need to come from previous work experiences. They can relate to a personal experience, sports, family, community or volunteer activities.

In order to tell the story effectively, you will want to outline the following:

- Your goal; what you wanted to accomplish
- The obstacle, difficulty or challenge you faced
- A brief description of what you did step-by-step
- A summary of the outcome
- Any quantifiable result attributable to your actions

You will probably want to write out examples of how you have used at least four or five different skills so that you are ready to interject a brief story in answer to an interviewer's questions. Among other advantages, this approach will allow you to stand out in the mind of the interviewer and will imprint your skills on his/her memory.

DETERMINING YOUR PERSONAL AND PROFESSIONAL GOALS

In addition to evaluating your strengths and assessing what you have to offer a company, this is an opportune time to do a little soul searching regarding what you want to get out of your next position. The exercises on pages 10, 11 and 12 of this chapter should be helpful in this process.

This might be the time to consider starting your own business, making a career change, or going back to school. What is it you have always dreamed of doing? Is this the time to do it? Start by answering the following questions:

FINANCIAL

- What is your current financial situation? How long can you afford to go without a job?

- If you took on a temporary assignment, free-lance work or a part-time job, would it ease your financial burden enough to give you the time to find the RIGHT job?

- What are your financial objectives? Could you consider a position that pays less than you were previously earning, but has the potential of paying substantially more down the road (or involves an equity position in the company?)

- Is it essential that you receive medical benefits as part of your compensation package or do you have access to acceptable, affordable coverage through a family member? An association?

- Do you have the financial resources to start your own business? If you become a consultant or free-lancer, do you have other sources of income or sufficient savings to support you without a regular paycheck?

- Could you live on less money if you were in a job you loved? How much less could you afford to make?

- Would you take a position in your industry at a lower salary and managerial level if it afforded you more time to focus on other parts of your life?

TIME

- How many hours a week are you willing or able to devote to your next position?

- What are the other areas of your life that you want or need to devote time to? How much time?

· Family	· Travel/Weekend or Vacation Home
· Hobbies/Sports	· Continuing Education
· Volunteer Activities	· Other Interests/Commitments

- Would you enjoy working part-time and reducing your expenditure for childcare by caring for your children part-time?

- How much time are you willing to spend commuting? Would you take a lower level job if it were closer to home and could substantially reduce or eliminate your commute?

- Would you consider a relocation to be closer to your job?

LONG-RANGE GOALS

- How long do you want to be in your next position? Your next company?

- Are you contemplating retirement? How soon?

- Do you plan to relocate eventually for your retirement or another personal reason? Would you consider moving now?

- Do you ultimately want to change careers? If so, what are the reasons not to do so now?

- What would you have to change/sacrifice in order to make a career change now?

- Which of your interests or avocations would you love to turn into a vocation or new career?

Perhaps you have reached a plateau in your career and feel that it might be worth exploring other opportunities. This could be the time to pursue different career paths and see what opportunities arise. While you are looking for a job in your current field of expertise, you may also want to explore possibilities in other areas where you have a strong interest, but no practical experience.

Career changes are not for everyone, of course. It is important to answer all of the questions above and many more before deciding to take the plunge. Not everyone is cut out to be an entrepreneur or to deal with the uncertainties of consulting or free-lance work. It is crucial when you are contemplating a change to network with people who are doing what you want to do. Ask them what it takes to be successful and then ask yourself if you have what it takes.

In the last few years a number of executives in the fashion industry have pursued their dreams and applied their skills and talents to new careers.

- *One woman with a 20+ year retail merchandising career went to cooking school and is now a chef in a three-star restaurant in the Berkshires where she had a vacation home.*

- *Another fashion executive, with an extensive background in luxury goods and fashion accessories marketing, turned an interest into a business. She designs web sites for fashion and consumer package goods companies.*

- *A design director for a sportswear manufacturer applied his knowledge of merchandising and color to a highly successful interior design business.*

- *An executive with a major pattern company translated her fashion merchandising experience into a management position in a home furnishings fabric company.*

WHAT IS IMPORTANT TO ME?

In this exercise, your objective is to examine your likes and dislikes, strengths and weaknesses and what you desire in a job situation. Your task is to write down as many different answers as you can, either positive or negative, as long as they accurately reflect what is important to you. *(E.g.: "I need to work with other people. I am not as productive working independently." or "I like to work in a high-pressure, fast-paced environment with very bright people." or "I thrive in an unstructured, creative environment." or "I want a situation that will allow me the flexibility to spend more time with my family.")* You should consider what makes you feel good about yourself, what you find fulfilling, what motivates you and what, other than work, is an important part of your life.

RANK	STATEMENT

Working with the descriptions you have just listed, put "1" in the RANK column next to the statement which reflects what you feel is the most important. Next, number the other statements in the RANK column to indicate their relative rank of importance.

Having done this, think about the types of companies and positions that might satisfy these criteria.

WHO'S WHO

In the space below, write a short statement about yourself as it might appear in a listing of important people. Be descriptive rather than judgmental, but don't be humble.

_____

_____

_____

_____

_____

_____

HIDDEN GOALS

Somewhere within each of us there are hidden goals we would like to reach, goals that generally are not known by other people. These goals may remain hidden because they seem unattainable. In this exercise, your task is to describe an ideal job you would like to have before you stop working. This description should include your hidden goals.

_____

_____

_____

_____

_____

NOTE: If you need more space for your answers to this and the following questions, use a separate sheet of paper.

Identify the skills that apply to you e.g. communications ability, financial acumen, strong negotiator. Then fill in the chart below to sort those skills into the three categories. This will enable you to begin focusing on the responsibilities you would like to have and the skills you would want to use in your next position. The Action Verbs List on the following page may help to remind you of some of your skills. It will also help you write an effective resume.

SKILL	(✓) CAN DO	(✓) DO BETTER THAN MOST	(✓) LIKE TO DO

ACTION VERBS (Skills)

accelerated	enlarged	operated	sparked
accommodated	established	optimized	spearheaded
accomplished	expanded	organized	spurred
acclimated	expedited	originated	staffed
acquired	facilitated	oversaw	stabilized
achieved	focused	performed	started
administered	forecast	pinpointed	streamlined
advised	formulated	planned	strengthened
analyzed	founded	presented	stressed
approved	generated	prevented	stretched
arranged	governed	prioritized	structured
assumed	grouped	processed	succeeded
authorized	guided	progressed	summarized
broadened	headed	produced	superseded
budgeted	hiked	profiled	supervised
built	identified	profited	surpassed
capitalized	implemented	programmed	sustained
cataloged	improved	promoted	systematized
collaborated	improvised	propelled	targeted
completed	inaugurated	proposed	taught
compiled	increased	provided	terminated
conceived	installed	purchased	traced
conducted	instituted	recognized	tracked
contributed	instructed	recommended	traded
consolidated	insured	recruited	trained
contracted	interacted	redesigned	transferred
controlled	interfaced	reduced	transformed
converted	intensified	reorganized	translated
created	introduced	researched	trimmed
decreased	invented	reshaped	tripled
defined	investigated	restructured	uncovered
delivered	launched	revamped	unified
demonstrated	led	revised	unraveled
designed	lessened	revitalized	used
developed	maintained	saved	utilized
devised	managed	scheduled	vacated
directed	maneuvered	serviced	verified
distributed	maximized	set up	widened
doubled	merged	simplified	withdrew
earned	minimized	slashed	won
edited	moderated	sold	worked
eliminated	monitored	solved	wrote
enhanced	negotiated	sorted	

IMMEDIATE GOALS

Now that you have considered your long-term goals and assessed your skills and personal preferences, it is time to think about your immediate goals. Which specific positions are best suited to your talents and experience and which companies would you be most interested in working for? Answering these questions or at least setting some initial goals will help you focus both your resume and personal presentation.

One of the problems many people encounter at this stage of the search process is that they are unsure specifically of what they want to do next and feel a need to keep their options open. Unfortunately, this can result in a wishy-washy presentation. *Focus* should be your priority.

> *A fashion executive we know was working for a "hot" new designer company. She received numerous calls every week from people interested in working for the company. When asked what position they were interested in, a number of people replied "I don't care. I'll do anything." These are the callers whose names and numbers went immediately into the wastebasket. Their lack of focus was a total turnoff to the potential employer.*

Had an applicant said "I am interested in a sales management position" or "I feel I could contribute to the public relations effort," the executive would have kept her name on file or even agreed to a personal meeting. It is not unusual, particularly in a young and growing company, for a person whose experience is in one area to be considered for an entirely different position.

The executive in the example above actually came to the company this way herself. She was speaking with the designer about creating a direct mail catalog business and ended up as the Director of Public Relations and Advertising for the company!

> *The lesson here is that a focus will* not *limit your option; it* will *help you present yourself in a professional and intelligent manner.*

For some people it will be easier to target *specific positions* and then research the companies that might have opportunities in this area. For others, it may be preferable to focus on the *specific companies* that might be a good fit and then research the job opportunities that match their particular qualifications.

As your search progresses, your job and company specifications will evolve. Don't fixate on them. Think of this process as part of an outline for an overall Job Search Strategy. We'll develop the strategy in Chapter IV.

TARGET POSITIONS

List below the positions you are seeking, based on your qualifications and experience. Keep in mind that the specific job title will vary from company to company and will often depend on the size of the organization. For example, a Vice-President of Merchandising in a $20 million company might be equivalent to a Product Manager in a $100 million company.

_____	_____
_____	_____
_____	_____
_____	_____
_____	_____
_____	_____
_____	_____

TARGET COMPANIES

List the companies you think would offer opportunities appropriate to your goals. If you are changing careers or industries, list the type of companies that might benefit from your prior experience. For example, if your background is in the cosmetics industry, you may want to target fashion accessory manufacturers, catalog companies and/or brand name active sportswear and sporting goods companies that could also use your expertise in marketing consumer package goods.

INDUSTRY #1	INDUSTRY #2	INDUSTRY #3
_____	_____	_____
_____	_____	_____
_____	_____	_____
_____	_____	_____
_____	_____	_____
_____	_____	_____
_____	_____	_____

NOTES:

CHAPTER III

DEVELOPING A DYNAMIC RESUME

It is important to remember that your resume is a door opener — it won't get you the job, but it can get you in the door to interview for one. At the same time, a poorly written resume can exclude you immediately.

You should read this section even if you have a current resume. The information that follows will help you polish what you have already written and develop your resume into a key component of your marketing strategy. Think of your resume as a marketing tool. As with any promotional material, the object is to stand out from the competition.

Will your resume survive a 30-second scan?

Anyone who receives a great many resumes will tell you that they do not really read them. What will catch their eye in 30 seconds? Most will tell you that numbers do; *the more you are able to quantify your accomplishments, the better.*

CHRONOLOGICAL VS. FUNCTIONAL RESUMES

You will note that all of the sample resumes we have included are in the *chronological* format. Although many resume guides include functional resumes (where a person's experience is grouped by skills and functions rather than by employment history) we do not recommend using that format. Executive recruiters, many human resource professionals, and other executives who hire at a management level agree that a functional resume sends up a red flag.

A functional resume often indicates that the person is trying to hide a weakness in their experience, e.g. a lengthy time period between jobs, too many job changes in a short period of time, or other inconsistencies in a person's work history. Even if you are planning to make a career change, a well-written chronological resume is the preferred format. Your transferable skills will still be readily evident to the reader.

FORMAT STYLE

The format of the resume should not be too creative. The sample resumes at the end of this chapter will give you an idea of how yours could look. You can vary the font but *be sure to use an easily readable font size so that the recipient does not have to strain to read it.* The resume should be printed or photocopied on white or ivory paper. If you need to fax it, any other color will come through badly.

A two-page resume is perfectly acceptable. Just be sure that the most current information is included on the first page, (i.e., your employers during the last 5-8 years.) For students seeking an entry-level position or job seekers with less than 5-8 years of experience, a one-page resume is preferable. Do not reduce the font size in order to squeeze the information onto one or two pages. Edit!

A TWO-PAGE RESUME IS PERFECTLY ACCEPTABLE. ANYTHING LONGER IS NOT.

We recommend starting the resume with a **Career Summary**. Starting with an objective may limit your opportunities. It is easier to create this summary after you have written the rest of the resume so we will return to it later in this chapter.

THE WORK HISTORY

After your name, address, telephone numbers, e-mail address (you would be surprised how many people forget these) and your career summary, the reader will look for the *companies* you have worked for, the *dates* at those companies and your *job titles*. Keep in mind the following when you are writing these down:

1) Dates should encompass the entire time you were employed by a particular company. Only the years are necessary, not the months. If you held several positions within one company, those dates should be indicated in parentheses after each position.

2) If you have worked for small to medium-sized companies, lesser known companies, or if you are considering a career change, describe the company's business, product, volume, etc.

3) If your title is obscure or carries with it atypical responsibilities, give a brief description of what it means. For example, "Product Manager" or "Account Executive" can mean entirely different things in different companies.

A brief *job description* should follow. Remember — *be concise and look at the big picture.* Try to include only the responsibilities relevant to someone who will want to hire you, i.e., managerial and decision-making functions. The daily administrative tasks that may take up much of your time are not managerial functions, e.g., sending faxes, record keeping, coordinating schedules, etc.

ACCOMPLISHMENTS

After the basic outline of your work history, you will need to tackle the substance of the resume — your accomplishments. This is where it is important to think about *quantifying* what you have done and documenting your achievements in a memorable way. *This is not the time to be humble, shy or vague.*

• Think about areas where you brought about volume increases. What were they?

_____

_____

• You improved productivity. By how much?

_____

_____

• How many people did you hire, manage and/or train?

_____

_____

• How large was the budget you administered?

_____

_____

Read the examples of accomplishment statements on the following pages to assist you in formulating your own.

We can break these accomplishment statements down even further by looking at the key word at the beginning of each sentence or phrase: *created, increased, conceptualized* — all action verbs.

There are two phrases that often appear on resumes that are *NOT* action verbs — *coordinated* and *responsible for*. Neither of these terms does justice to what you are trying to get across. There is always a stronger way to rephrase it with an action verb. Refer back to the Action Verbs List in Chapter II.

SAMPLE ACCOMPLISHMENT STATEMENTS

- Prepared and managed $15 million divisional budget.

- Reduced overtime 50% by systematizing reports and schedules.

- Developed and implemented company-wide account executive performance standards.

- Promoted from Sales Representative to Account Executive after 6 months.

- Created and conducted training programs for store associates, resulting in enhanced product knowledge and customer service.

- Conceptualized and executed line of better-priced handbags, resulting in $6 million of new sales the first year.

- Increased sportswear division volume from $27 to $42 million in first two years.

- Profit and sales increases ranked in top 3 of 20 divisions.

- Upgraded computer systems in sales department to facilitate tracking of sales data and projections

- Launched XYZ dress division that grew to $12 million in first year.

- Built Active Swimwear area from inception to $27 million annual volume with 50% gross margin.

- Conceived of and created innovative product for import program projected to achieve $15 million in sales in 3 years.

- Hired, trained and supervised staff of 60 sales associates in 9 stores.

- As sole designer, conceptualized, merchandised and designed line from inception to $12 million volume in 4 years.

- Traveled extensively in 23 countries overseas and opened 2 new foreign markets.

- Realized 10% net profit on $4.5 million annual retail sales of Active Sportswear.

- Chosen to train newly appointed supervisors in management and leadership techniques.

- Identified cost reduction opportunities for printing and color separation, resulting in savings of over $250,000 a year.

- Exceeded sales objectives 7 out of 7 years by 3% to 28%.

(Sample Accomplishment Statements continued)

- Met salary and other expense targets for all projects.

- Planned and conducted semi-annual sales meetings for 50 sales representatives and regional managers.

- Instituted a management reporting system that was adopted as the corporate standard for all divisions.

- Developed new quality control standards and wrote Q.C. guidelines handbook for company.

- Created dramatic new image for sportswear ads, resulting in heightened consumer awareness and increased sales.

- Received Marketing Excellence Award for creative copy (awarded by peers)

- Eliminated cost of outside studios, resulting in $600,000 annual savings.

- Prepared major study that resulted in increased licensing fees, leading to $1 million profit from break-even in one year.

- Directed 4 departments with 90 professional and technical people.

- Analyzed regional demographics and developed new marketing strategy generating over $400,000 in additional sales.

- Planned and scheduled production of 5,000 new designs a year through 50 factories in 8 countries.

- Increased volume 23% by improving operating procedures, raising customer service standards and motivating sales associates with better incentives.

- Led Coats & Suits and Intimate Apparel to the 1st and 2nd net operating positions in the company, resulting in a promotion to SVP/General Merchandise Manager in 2001.

- Redefined and refocused the Retail Sales Coordinator program to be revenue driven, effecting a 20% retail sales increase over previous year.

- Introduced new practices in technology to support design and processes, including CAD system and Gerber cutting and sewing applications.

- Eliminated or streamlined non-performing product categories and created new private label categories causing a 50% increase in private label sales to J.C. Penney and WalMart.

YES, YOU CAN!

You may be saying to yourself: *"Well that may apply to someone else, but my job was different. I can't use those words or quantify with numbers. They don't apply to what I did."* or *"I don't know the exact figures."* You **can** come up with hard quantifiable data if you think about it.

Think back to something you did 5 years ago or for another company. Did you devise a new way of doing something subsequently adopted by the company for so long that you would not think to take credit for its initial development?

You may want to ask former co-workers or a friend or relative whether something that you accomplished, or your department achieved, stands out in their minds.

Certainly, you will have accomplishments that you will want to include that cannot be measured in numbers, such as:

- *Developed new program* (which has not yet had any results)
- *Chaired task force.*
- *Wrote training manual.*

You can even quantify your intent:

- *Designed and implemented new computerized scheduling system projected to reduce overtime hours by 20%.*
- *Instituted sales incentive program designed to increase productivity by 25%.*

Don't worry about tooting your own horn or bragging. It is not necessary to over-exaggerate your achievements, but this is the time to enumerate them. There is no advantage in being modest when you are trying to sell yourself.

THE CAREER SUMMARY

Now that you have identified your skills and accomplishments, it should be easier to write the introduction to your resume. Keep in mind that you do not want to incorporate everything you have done in your career in a lengthy paragraph. This is an opportunity to *highlight the important skills and experience* you have acquired. On the following pages, you will find some examples of Career Summaries to help you develop your own.

CAREER SUMMARY SAMPLES

- Ten years of progressively responsible positions in apparel merchandising and product development. Expertise in domestic and import fabric markets, line planning, costing and piece goods negotiations. Detail-oriented with strong analytical and organizational abilities.

- Accomplished marketing executive with experience in public relations, sales promotion, advertising and direct marketing. Successful problem solver with unique combination of creative and management skills.

- Creative and versatile design director with extensive experience in women's sportswear and dresses. Knowledge of worldwide fabric markets as well as import and domestic production. Experienced in all phases of line planning and execution.

- Twenty-three years of successful leadership and management experience in sales and marketing of Men's and Boys' Apparel. Proven ability to effect consistent volume and bottom-line increases. Experience in hiring, training and motivating sales staff.

- Fifteen years of diversified management experience in increasingly responsible positions involving national marketing of branded products. Highly developed strategic planning and organizational skills. Excellent interpersonal and communications abilities.

- Experienced retail merchandising executive with over twenty years of progressively responsible positions in major department and specialty store corporate offices. Achieved salary and other expense targets for all projects. Traveled extensively to 23 countries in Europe, the Far East and South America.

- Apparel manufacturing professional with broad experience in numerous women's and children's wear product categories. Areas of expertise include: sourcing, costing, price negotiations, production planning and scheduling. Ability to communicate effectively with design and sales and interpret their needs in product execution.

- Experienced communications professional skilled in creating and implementing programs to increase visibility and enhance image of businesses. Superior writing, management and organizational abilities.

(Career Summary Samples continued)

- Marketing Manager with fifteen years of in-depth experience in fragrance industry. Areas of expertise include: promotion, product development and market research. Excellent management and staff development skills; proven ability to adapt to rapidly changing conditions.

- Extensive, hands-on experience in managing public relations communication programs with Fortune 500 company. Strong interpersonal, administrative and communication skills demonstrated through progressively greater management responsibilities.

- Professional manager with extensive experience in marketing and product management. Successful problem solver with strategic planning, organizational and administrative skills.

- Nineteen years of progressively responsible positions in program management and development, planning and research including:

  · Program design/management/evaluation   · Project management
  · Short-term and long-term planning   · Competition analysis
  · Budget development and control   · Research/data analysis

(DRAFT YOUR CAREER SUMMARY BELOW IN THE SPACE PROVIDED)

_____

_____

_____

_____

_____

_____

_____

_____

_____

EDUCATIONAL/PERSONAL EXPERIENCE

Do not forget to include your educational background and any professional development workshops and courses you have completed. It is not necessary to include educational information prior to college.

If you do not have a degree but attended college, write down the dates you were there. It is a good idea to include the dates of your undergraduate as well as graduate degrees. Executive recruiters and other personnel professionals may think that by omitting them you are trying to hide something.

If you choose to include outside activities, think of the affiliations that will help sell you to an employer or which might make a connection with the person reading the resume, e.g.:

- Trade association memberships
- Community service activities or volunteer work
- Directorships of companies or organizations

It is a good idea to avoid political or religious affiliations or activities as they might alienate the reader. Your date of birth, health, physical description, Social Security number and marital status do not need to be included in the resume. It is also not necessary to say "references available upon request." Of course they are!

RESUME CHECK LIST

☑ Does your resume pass the 30-second scan?
☑ Did you use the chronological resume format?
☑ How does your career summary read?
☑ Did you quantify your accomplishments?
☑ Are company names, dates and business descriptions clear?
☑ Are you using strong action verbs?
☑ Did you include relevant education information?
☑ Is the font easily readable?

REMEMBER:

 Numbers – Short Sentences – Action Verbs – Crisp & Clear Company Descriptions!

The form on the following pages can be used to draft your resume. It may be useful to make copies of the form so that you can write several drafts. Be sure to make extra copies of the third page for other previous employers.

NOTES:

CHRONOLOGICAL RESUME FORMAT

Name _____

Address _____

City, State, Zip Code _____

Home Telephone _____

E-mail Address _____

CAREER SUMMARY

_____

_____

_____

_____

_____

_____

_____

_____

_____

_____

_____

_____

_____

_____

CAREER HISTORY

Most Recent Employer _____   Date: From_____To_____

Location, City, State _____

Position/Title _____

Brief Overview of Position _____

_____

_____

_____

_____

_____

_____

_____

Accomplishment Statements (Start with Verbs)

_____

_____

_____

_____

_____

_____

Employer #2_____   Date: From _____   To _____

Location, City, State _____

Position/Title _____

Brief Overview of Position _____

_____

_____

_____

_____

_____

_____

_____

_____

_____

Accomplishment Statements (Start with Verbs)

_____

_____

_____

_____

_____

_____

Employer #3_____ Date: From _____To_____

Location, City, State_____

Position/Title _____

Brief Overview of Position

_____

_____

_____

_____

_____

_____

_____

_____

_____

_____

_____

Accomplishment Statements (Start with Verbs)

_____

_____

_____

_____

_____

_____

_____

EDUCATION & PROFESSIONAL DEVELOPMENT

Degree/Diploma/Certificate _____Date _____

School Name, City, State _____

Other Relevant Training such as Language Skills, Computer Skills, etc

_____

_____

_____

_____

MILITARY SERVICE (OPTIONAL)

Classification _____

Branch, Year _____

PROFESSIONAL AND COMMUNITY AFFILIATIONS

Position, Name of Organization _____

Position, Name of Organization _____

Position, Name of Organization _____

Position, Name of Organization _____

Position, Name of Organization _____

CATHERINE FASHION
4825 Leavenworth St. #5B
San Francisco, CA 94109
Tel. 415 323-1414
Fax 415 323-1415
E-mail: cfashion@yahoo.com

SUMMARY

Experienced and highly regarded Design Director for Better Sportswear collections. Ability to motivate design team in creation of innovative yet functional design and inspire excellence in execution. Ability to create synergy between product, marketing and brand orientation.

PROFESSIONAL EXPERIENCE

LEVI STRAUSS AND CO.   **May 2001 to Present**
San Francisco, CA

Creative/Design Director, Dockers

Creative responsibility for the overall development and approval of the Men's, Women's and Boys' collections and all licensee products with a total annual volume of $980 million. Manage staff of 26 designers, product developers and merchandisers.

- Developed creative concept and marketing strategy for "Dockers K-1 Khakis" program that achieved record sell-through in test stores.
- Instituted new merchandising strategy to satisfy more active customer lifestyle trends resulting in 14% sales increase in first season.
- Implemented a "brand segmentation" strategy identifying key distinctions between product, packaging, distribution and marketing for all Dockers lines.
- Introduced new work practices in product development and offshore sourcing resulting in substantial savings for company.
- Collaborate with all licensees and approve all licensee product lines and marketing initiatives.

NAUTICA   **1992 to 2001**
New York

Vice President of Design and Merchandising – Outerwear, Swimwear, Bottoms and Nautica Competition (1994-1999)

Directed all aspects of the development, design and integration of the outerwear, bottoms, swimwear and Competition lines. Managed design room and product development team.

- Worked closely with Founder/President in design, development and evolution of Nautica Sportswear and Nautica Competition, growing volume from $45M to $475 million.
- Collaborated with sales, marketing and licensees on integration of seasonal concepts and new initiatives.
- Effected consistent annual and seasonal sales growth in all categories.
- Traveled extensively to the Far East and Europe for production, line development, market research and trade fairs.

NAUTICA (continued)
Head Designer – Outerwear, Bottoms and Swimwear (1992-1996)
- Established and developed strong design product development and technical support departments needed to execute sportswear collection.
- Created Nautica bottoms line, establishing standards of design, fabrication and fit, building category into a $50 million annual business.

ESPRIT, San Francisco, CA   **1990-1992**

Designer, Esprit "Hi-Summer" line
- Designed collection of junior knit and woven tops and bottoms.
- Assisted Suzie Thompkins on special design projects for Esprit Kids and Jeans collections.

CALVIN KLEIN SPORT   **1988-1990**
New York, NY
Associate Designer (1989-1990)
Assistant Designer (1988-1989)

EDUCATION

Parsons School of Design, Fashion Design, B.F.A., 1988

MICHAEL MERCHANT
555 East 55th Street
New York, NY 10019
Tel. (212) 765-4321/Fax 212 765-4320
E-mail mikemerchant@nyc.rr.com

SUMMARY

Experienced hands-on merchandising executive with unique ability to blend creative aspects of design direction with profit-oriented business strategy. Extensive domestic and international experience in fabric sourcing and product development. Talent for developing fabrics that look expensive but are well-priced, saleable and profitable.

PROFESSIONAL EXPERIENCE

CITY DKNY, Division of Liz Claiborne, Inc. New York, NY   **2002 - Present**
Director of Product Development, Wovens, Knits & Sweaters
Launched the product development department for this new women's sportswear licensee. Full responsibility for all fabric research and development, including negotiating price and all minimum/lead times. Established all operating procedures.

- Hired and trained product development team of 6 to translate design team's vision into a marketable collection.
- Instrumental in building volume growth from zero to $85 million.
- Researched and developed fabrics at target price points meeting initial mark-up goals.
- Set up highly effective pre-costing garment system.
- Traveled extensively to Europe and the Orient to attend fabric shows, for fabric research and development, and to build relationships with vendors and mills.

THE LIMITED, New York, NY   **2000-2002**
Director of Fabric Research and Development
Directed global fabric research in all apparel classifications for this $700 million company. Sourced in the Far East, Europe, Mexico, Central America and the U.S. Selected mills and vendors. Supervised team of fabric managers and coordinators. Worked closely with in-house design team to create consistent aesthetic image.

- Co-launched and developed the "Virtual Stretch System" which now accounts for 70% of The Limited's volume. Identified new fabric qualities in various blends, creating a total separates collection with an updated, refined look. This successful program which had never previously been utilized at this price point, contributed to returning the company to profitability in under two years.

CK CALVIN KLEIN, New York, NY   **1996-2000**
Director of Fabric Sourcing and Purchasing, Women's Division
Directed global sourcing in Far East, Europe, Latin America, and the U.S. Worked closely with design team in all phases of product development.
- Instituted and built entire fabric department and reestablished mill base to support growth from $30 million to $70 million.
- Recruited and trained fabric managers and coordinators.
- Researched and purchased exclusive highest quality fabrics at low cost, successfully achieving target price points.

INTERNATIONAL WOMEN'S APPAREL, New York, NY   **1993-1996**
Fabric Stylist/Merchandiser M.M. by Krizia and Austin Reid divisions

COUNTERPARTS, INC., New York, NY   **1989-1993**
Fabric Merchandiser/Piece Goods Buyer

EDUCATION AND TRAINING
A.A.S., Fashion Design, Fashion Institute of Technology, New York, 1989

Camille College
camille.college@drexeluniv.edu

275 Ridgefield Road
Allentown, Pa. 60960
610-625-8837

Box 2819
Drexel University
Philadelphia, PA 60543
215-697-5037

SKILLS SUMMARY

Bright, energetic, soon-to-graduate student with outstanding organizational and administrative skills. Able to work independently, synthesize information and concepts and be a productive team member. Experience in retail and wholesale. Excellent computer skills.

EDUCATION

DREXEL UNIVERSITY, Philadelphia, PA   **2001-Present**
Bachelor of Science in Design & Merchandising anticipated June 2004. GPA 3.26

EMPLOYMENT EXPERIENCE

NICOLE MILLER, Philadelphia, PA   **January-May 2004**
Wholesale Showroom, Showroom Assistant
- Placed orders and authorized returns for wholesale accounts
- Organized wholesale showroom, prioritized collection by delivery date and availability
- Developed bridal resource book for over 200 accounts, increasing sales by 10%
- Communicated with corporate office divisions

Retail Designer Boutique, Sales Associate
- Built personal client relations through preference profiling systems
- Achieved andexceeded high sales goals: approximately $40K in sales

OLD NAVY—DIVISION OF GAP, Freehold, NJ   **Summers 2001-04**
Sales Associate
- Interpreted and executed visual merchandising plans from corporate office
- Maintained client relations while generating high sales for the store
- Operated point of sale system for multi-million dollar store

COMPUTER EXPERIENCE

- Operating Systems: IBM and MAC
- Software: Microsoft Word, Microsoft Excel, Microsoft Power Point, Adobe Illustrator, Adobe Photoshop, Quark, AS400

HONORS AND ACTIVITIES

Member Philadelphia Advertising Club, President Phi Mu Sorority, Dean's List, Fashion Show Production, Fashion Show Dresser

YVETTE YOUNG
yvetteyoung@aol.com
280 East 79th Street, Apt. F
New York, New York 10004
212-871-6392

SUMMARY

Creative and versatile designer with exceptional sense of style. Excellent skills include impeccable flat sketching and clear, detailed illustrations. Highly proficient in CAD. Outstanding interpersonal and communications abilities.

EXPERIENCE

Nautica International, Inc., New York, NY   **2003-present**
Better sportswear manufacturer
Assistant Designer
Assist in all aspects of design for men's swimwear and hats.
- Create all flat sketches and CAD color boards.
- Develop complete prototype packages.
- Handle detail sheets, daily overseas communication and follow-up.
- Assist in fabric sourcing.
- Approve print strike offs, trims and graphics

Authentic Fitness Corp. Los Angeles, CA   **2002-2003**
Men's and women's active sportswear manufacturer
Assistant Designer, Women's Fashion and Performance Swimwear
Participated in design layout, fitting sessions, pattern development and sewing process for Ralph Lauren, Oscar de la Renta, Speedo, Victoria's Secret and Catalina swimwear lines.

Fashion International, Los Angeles, CA   **2001**
Fashion show production company
Internship
Assisted in assembling and styling contemporary and better women's fashions for televised charity fashion show.

EDUCATION

Fashion Institute of Design and Merchandising (FIDM), Los Angeles, CA
A.A.S. Fashion Design, December 2002

Boston College, Newton, MA
B.A. Humanities, May 2001

COMPUTER SKILLS
Microsoft Word, Web Pdm, Excel, Power Point. Photoshop 6.0, Illustrator 9

SUSAN SELLER
60 Central Park West
New York, NY 10023
(212) 976-1212
E-mail suseller@aol.com

PROFESSIONAL PROFILE

Dynamic, experienced sales executive with proven track record of consistent volume increases in the Bridge and Designer markets. Proven success in turning around businesses by strengthening their foundation in sales, marketing, merchandising and profitability. Exceptional presentation and interpersonal skills. Excellent motivational and training abilities. Strong numbers orientation.

EXPERIENCE

1999 to Present
DANA BUCHMAN division of LIZ CLAIBORNE, INC
Vice President, Sales & Marketing
Directed sales for 3 divisions: Bridge Sportswear, Petites and Dresses. Managed sales staff of 14. Involved in product planning from budget phase to merchandising.
- Increased sportswear division volume from $87 million to $122 million in first 2+ years.
- Effected profit and sales increases that ranked in top 5 out of 34 divisions.
- Managed Saks Fifth Avenue account for all 3 divisions, achieving consistent double-digit percentage increases.
- Directed launch of Petite and Dress divisions.
- Negotiated with French, German and U.K. retail operations for European distribution.

1994-1999
ELLEN TRACY
National Sales Manager, Ellen Tracy Petites
- Launched Petites division for this manufacturer of bridge sportswear
- Built volume of Petite division to $45 million representing 32% of total volume.
- Hired and trained sales force.
- Negotiated retail space allocations with major department and specialty store chains.

1990-1994
CALVIN KLEIN, INC.
Regional Sales Manager, Calvin Klein Sport Division
- Directed sales for $70 million of $300 million casual sportswear division.
- Successfully repositioned line to bridge market.
- Increased gross profit by 8%.
- Computerized sales department to better manage sales data, tracking and sales projections.

1987 to 1990
CATHY HARDWICK
$20+ million manufacturer of better contemporary women's apparel.
Vice President of Sales & Merchandising
Directed contemporary bridge sportswear and dress divisions.
- Launched Cathy Hardwick dress division, achieving $5 million in first year.
- Managed major accounts including: Saks Fifth Avenue, Bloomingdale's, and Macy's.

1985 to 1987
BRITT AMERICA, Subsidiary of Miss Britt, Hamburg, Germany
Women's apparel manufacturer.
U.S. Sales Director
Launched designer sportswear line in U.S. market.

1983 to 1985
INTUITIONS SPORTSWEAR
Better women's sportswear manufacturer
Account Executive

EDUCATION

West Virginia University, Fashion Design/Business, B.S., 1983

PERSONAL

Member: The Fashion Group International; The National Association of Female Executives

ROBERT RETAILER
E-mail: robret@verizon.net
500 East 50th Street
New York, NY 10019
(212) 222-1111

SUMMARY

Results oriented merchandising executive with broad, diverse experience in retailing and manufacturing. Proven track record of developing and implementing strategies to increase sales, profit margins and inventory turnover. An exceptional leader, problem solver and decision maker.

EXPERIENCE

BROOKS BROTHERS, New York, NY   **2000 – Present**
Vice President , Men's Furnishings, Dress Shirts, Neckwear, Accessories & Shoes
Responsibility for sales, marketing, product development, strategic planning and operations.

- Trained, developed and managed team of 15 buyers, planners, and allocators.
- Increased markup by 1.3, dollar margin by 9.1% and sales by $586,000 over prior year. (1999)
- Introduced No Iron shirts and Average Sleeve Lengths which accounted for 48% of the Dress Shirt Sales.
- Converted major basic furnishings programs to quick response, EDI, and vendor supply chain using systems integration to improve sales and increase inventory turn 20%.
- Implemented new monthly merchandising guidelines for retail stores to improve productivity and customer service.

BLOOMINGDALE'S, New York, NY   **1993-2000**
Buyer, Dress Shirts (1994-1997)
Created and launched Italian private label better dress shirt collection increasing private label from 20% to 40% of $25 million dress shirt business.

Buyer, Men's Accessories (1990-1994)
Managed volume of $15 million

COACH LEATHERWARE, INC. New York, NY   **1989-1993**
Director, Product Development and Merchandising
Established product development department for manufacturer and retailer of women's and men's leather goods and accessories. Company grew from $25 million to $150 million between 1986 and 1990.

- Hired and managed staff of product managers, merchandisers, patternmakers, and designers.
- Developed new products accounting for 64% of total sales in 1990.
- Created new product lines including shoes, luggage, scarves, neckwear and watches.

R.H. MACY'S, INC., New York, NY   **1987-1989**
Buyer, Designer Handbags **(1987-1989)**
Volume $8 million
- Initiated first "Coach Shop" concept in a department store.
- Effected 25% sales increase in 1985.
- Created private label program in Italy and Orient increasing dollar margins by 5%.
Buyer, Fashion Accessories **(1985-87)**
Assistant Buyer, Junior Jeans **(1984-1985)**
Department Manager, Men's Clothing **(1983-1984)**

EDUCATION

Indiana University, Business/Marketing , B.S. 1982

Macy's Executive Training Program, 1979-1983

CHRISTINE CREATIVE

Christicreative@mindspring.com

300 East 54th Street
New York, NY 10022

212 873-2345 Home
212 682-4439 Office

SUMMARY

Creative executive with exceptional image, style and communications skills. Extensive experience in conversions and turnarounds. Crisis manager bringing organizational skills and logical decision making process to solve critical problems. Proven ability to handle multi-faceted projects simultaneously. Broad-based background in diversified industries including cosmetics, fragrance, fashion, tabletop and retail.

PROFESSIONAL EXPERIENCE

LANCASTER GROUP WORLDWIDE, New York, NY   **2003 – Present**
International manufacturer and marketer of prestige fragrances and cosmetics
Creative Director
Selected by management to establish and direct Creative Marketing Services Department.

- Direct and manage creative functions formerly performed by advertising agency, reducing development and production costs by 50%.
- Named, themed and positioned products, technologies and color stories including Lancaster Balanced Care Sunblock, Monteil Paris, Lancaster True-To-Life Color.
- Wrote public relations campaigns for European press presentation of Sculpture by Nikos Parfums and Chopard Heaven.
- Manage professional staff of 6 designers and coordinators.

LANCASTER GROUP USA, New York, NY   **2000-2003**
US marketing arm of international company
Creative Director

- Established, staffed and managed in-house Creative Services Department.
- Successfully launched 7 fragrances with two-person department.
- Identified suppliers, purchased art, print, collateral and novelty items in absence of purchasing department.
- Created and implemented in-store events such as Chopard Casmir "Safe Cracking" which generated over 10,000 customers in single week.
- Contributed to three consecutive years of record growth in which start-up company achieved sales of $120 million.

REVLON, New York, NY   1997-2000
$1.6 billion diversified cosmetic, health and beauty aid manufacturer and distributor
Co-Creative Director, Department Store Division
- Named, themed and positioned products, promotions, shades and events such as Germaine Monteil Habitat Makeup, Marine Therapie, Lightyears Eye Area Formula, entire range of new treatment, color and makeup products for Charles of the Ritz.
- Created gift-with-purchase items, directed manufacturers in fabrication and construction.
- Directed all graphics, production and copy of *Field Newsletter,* published and distributed quarterly by Beauty Fashion Magazine.
- Created and produced marketing books and field sales materials for bi-annual meetings.

CREATIVE CONSULTANT   1995-1997
- Developed advertising, public relations, direct marketing and sales promotion concepts for variety of accounts. Clients included Liz Claiborne, Lord & Taylor, Clinique Labs, Inc., Shoe Biz and Revlon.

CLINIQUE LABORATORIES, INC., New York, NY   1988-1992
Vice President, Creative Services
- Discovered and introduced Britt Hammer, the "face" of Clinique from 1985 to 1990.
- Redesigned in-house production procedures, reducing costs by 40% per season.
- Hired and managed professional staff of 10 copywriters and art directors.
- Created and executed copy concepts for national and retail print and broadcast advertising.

SAKS FIFTH AVENUE, New York, NY   1988-1992
Creative Director
- Conceptualized and implemented new fashion image and copy position awarded Retail Ad Week's Creative Image Award.
- Hired and managed creative staff of 20 print and video art directors, copywriters and fashion stylists.
- Obtained funding from major airlines and hotels to underwrite location shoots; traveled to Europe, North Africa and throughout US to direct execution of highly visible, award winning fashion campaigns such as Viewpoint: Paris, Moda Italia, Morocco! and SFA/USA: San Francisco.

AC&R ADVERTISING, New York, NY   1985-1988
Account Executive/Creative Contact

EDUCATION

Sarah Lawrence College, Bronxville, NY
B.A. Liberal Arts 1985

PROFESSIONAL AFFILIATIONS
Member - Cosmetic Executive Women, Fashion Group International

NOTES:

CHAPTER IV

JOB SEARCH STRATEGY AND TECHNIQUES

DEVELOPING A PERSONAL MARKETING PLAN

In order to make the best use of your time, it is important to restate your goals and focus your search toward attaining them. Use the form below to create a marketing plan for yourself based on the work you have done in Chapter II.

OBJECTIVE (What specific positions are you pursuing?)

_____

_____

_____

QUALIFICATIONS (What skills and experience will enable you to excel in these positions?)

_____

_____

_____

CONTRIBUTIONS (What are the specific areas you could contribute to and how?)

_____

_____

_____

LOCATION (Where would you like to work in order of preference?)

_____

_____

_____

CULTURE (What are the essential characteristics of an organization where you would like to work?)

_____

_____

_____

_____

TARGET COMPANIES/CONTACTS

(List the companies you listed in Chapter II and the name or title of the person you would ideally like to contact.) This list should be an ongoing one. Add extra pages so that you can continue to expand it.

COMPANY   CONTACT

_____   _____

_____   _____

_____   _____

_____   _____

_____   _____

_____   _____

_____   _____

_____   _____

On the next page you will find a sample marketing plan to help you develop your own.

SAMPLE PERSONAL MARKETING PLAN

OBJECTIVE
Design Director – Merchandiser/Designer – Design & Merchandising Consultant

QUALIFICATIONS
15 years of design experience for better and bridge sportswear manufacturers. Set up and staffed design studios. Traveled extensively throughout the Far East and South America working with contractors and company owned factories. Sourced and developed fabrics in Europe and the Far East

POTENTIAL CONTRIBUTIONS
Update and/or reposition line to reflect changing consumer tastes and lifestyles. Develop new fabric and print resources for company. Work with sales staffs to bring a unified effort to the development and marketing of line. Conceptualize and develop new casual wear or casual career line for company

LOCATION
New York
Might consider: Seattle, San Francisco

COMPANY CULTURE
Team oriented – Product driven – Forward thinking

TARGET COMPANIES/CONTACTS

Apparel Manufacturers

Finity	President/Division head
Liz Claiborne	Corp. V.P. Design
Jones Apparel Group	Division head or V.P. Merchandising
Anne Klein Group	President
Et Vous	President
Due Per Due	President
Nautica	President

Specialty Stores

Ann Taylor	GMM/VP
Talbots	President/VP/GMM
Banana Republic	VP Product/GMM

Catalogs

J. Crew	President/VP Merchandising

HOW PEOPLE ACTUALLY FIND JOBS

Networking 75%
Classified ads 4%
Internet job postings......................................7%
Search firms/employment agencies 8%
Other 6%

Looking for a job is a numbers game. When you send a resume in response to an ad in the newspaper or a web site job posting, you can safely assume that hundreds of other people will be responding as well. That is not to say it is not worth sending your resume and a well-written, targeted cover letter. It does mean that you should not be surprised if you do not receive a response.

When you look at the statistics, it is clear that the vast majority of your time should be spent networking. Since 25% of job seekers find employment by other means, however, you should pursue all of these methods.

Here are a few useful pointers about the non-networking approaches:

INTERNET JOB LISTINGS/EMPLOYMENT ADS

There are some excellent positions on the Internet and in help wanted ads today. Companies are less and less inclined to pay fees to agencies and recruiting firms, knowing that there are a lot of good people out there looking for opportunities. *Read the listings carefully*! If they ask for your current salary or a cover letter, they probably will not consider you if you don't comply.

On the Internet, each web site works differently. Many large manufacturers and retailers list current job openings that you can apply for directly on their web sites. If you don't see a job that interests you, some sites allow you to send a resume to be kept on file. On the web sites that act as clearing houses for many companies, such as Fashioncareercenter.com or Hotjobs.com,, you can apply for a specific job or post your resume in the hope that a potential employer will pick you out of the crowd. Many web sites give you the opportunity to search for job openings by job description as well as by company. If there is not a job opening that suits your experience, it may be worth searching target companies in order to get a sense of which ones are currently hiring.

Some web sites that specialize in a specific field such as fashion or retailing, offer the option of submitting your resume on a confidential basis. Only your fax number and e-mail address are given to the potential employer. If, for example, you are concerned about your current company learning that you are applying for a job with a competitor, this may be an option worth considering.

There are companies that require a cover letter that stays in their database. This is an excellent opportunity to utilize phrases from your Career Summary that reflect the attributes you want to communicate to the potential employer.

In some cases, such as Hotjobs.com, you are required to have an objective. It is not a good idea to make the objective too broad or vague. This only succeeds in making you look unfocused and may not contain the key words an employer is utilizing to screen resumes. Remember, you can always go back and change it if you find you are not getting the type of responses you are looking for.

Some career web sites require that you utilize their resume format. Often, you have the option of cutting and pasting pieces of your resume into their form or uploading an unformatted, plain text version of your resume. *Be aware! If you cut and paste your entire resume into the company's form or send it in the body of an e-mail, the resume will come through with no formatting and your carefully chosen font and layout will disappear.* Many companies offer you the opportunity to fax your resume if you want it to be received in the exact form in which you have written it. There are some companies that ask for your resume to be sent as an e-mail attachment. In this case, be sure you have written it in a commonly used word processing program so it can be opened on the other end.

> **For any Internet job, search carefully and read the requirements for sending in your qualifications. You do not want your resume to be deleted because it was sent incorrectly or appeared as indecipherable gobbledygook!**

If you know which company has placed a job listing and you haven't heard from them after several weeks, you may want to try to follow up with a telephone call. This is most effective if you know someone affiliated with the company. After sending your resume, call the person and ask what he knows about the position and if he might put in a good word for you. If your contact is a senior level executive in the company, you may want to ask for a personal introduction to the hiring executive.

EXECUTIVE RECRUITERS/SEARCH FIRMS

It is okay to e-mail or fax your resume to recruiters, but do not expect responses. You need to keep in mind that these firms are hired and paid by companies to fill specific positions. If they have an opportunity for you, you will hear from them. Don't be surprised if someone who tried to recruit you last year doesn't have time for you now. If you can develop a good rapport with a recruiter or are helpful with referrals, he may be more receptive to speaking with you even if he doesn't have an appropriate opportunity at the moment. Do not expect a great deal of interest from recruiters if you are trying to make a career change. Remember, they are hired to find people with the *specific experience* their client requires. It is rare for a search firm to have a client who asks for experience in a different field.

It is a good idea to use personal referrals to contact recruiters who work in your industry. If they have time, they may schedule a get-acquainted interview (particularly if the person who referred you is a client!) If you make a good impression, when an opportunity does come along, the recruiter may think of you before conducting a full-fledged search for additional candidates. If you do have a courtesy interview, remember that it was a courtesy and write a thank-you note to the recruiter as well as the person who referred you.

> **Keep in mind that executive recruiters are paid by companies to fill specific positions.**

NEVER PAY A FEE!

The legitimate recruiters are paid by the companies that hire them. It is unethical to take a fee from the candidate as well!

Some firms work on a *Retainer* basis – they are paid part of their fee up front and normally have the assignment exclusively. Other firms work on *Contingency* – they are paid only when the assignment is filled. Many recruiters who work in the fashion industry handle both types of assignments.

From time to time, contingency firms may send out unsolicited resumes to companies for whom they would like to work. It is a good idea to ask them to discuss all positions with you *before* they submit your resume. This will help you to avoid unpleasant incidents such as having your resume sent to a company you have already contacted or having two different recruiters submit your resume to the same company. (Companies will sometimes disqualify a candidate if this occurs, rather than have to worry about which firm gets the fee.)

If you post your resume on an Internet job site, do not be surprised if you receive a response from a company that sounds like a search firm and requests a meeting with you. When you ask for information as to the purpose of the meeting, you may find out that it is not a recruiter at all but rather a "Career Management" firm. These companies, which systematically search resumes posted on the web for executive level job seekers, offer to market you to potential employers for a substantial up front fee.

TARGET COMPANY LETTERS

Be sure you do sufficient RESEARCH before writing or e-mailing targeted companies. Visit company web sites wherever possible. Keep track of companies you have written and the individuals to whom you have addressed the letters. Every letter should be followed up by a phone call within 10 days. Be sure you have the correct spelling of the name and title of the person to whom your letter was sent. Send only as many letters as you can follow up on in a timely manner.

> **Research company thoroughly before writing.**
> —
> **Follow up with phone call.**
> —
> **Be sure to have correct spelling of names & titles.**
> —
> **Send only as many letters as you can follow up on.**

NETWORKING: THE POWER OF PERSONAL CONTACTS

A TRUE STORY: Susannah, a young woman we know, who had spent her first few years out of college working in Colorado, decided to return to New York where she grew up. In the course of looking for a job she contacted a former classmate who was working for an apparel company. When Susannah mentioned that she was looking for a marketing position her friend said that she knew of an opening in her company and would ask about it. She spoke to the Marketing Director who was the hiring executive and said that she had a friend with marketing experience who would be interested in the job. The Marketing Director said she had listed the job on the Internet and had received over 500 responses. She wanted to meet Susannah immediately because she did not want to read through all of those resumes! She interviewed Susannah and hired her two days later.

With the advent of Internet job listings and the use of e-mail and faxes to send resumes, hiring executives are receiving 4 to 5 times the number of responses to jobs as they had in the past. Susannah's boss is not the only one who found the prospect of weeding through hundreds of resumes daunting. It is more important than ever to utilize your contacts to help you stand out from the crowd.

UTILIZING CONTACTS

The criterion for a contact is simple: that he or she recognizes your name, (sometimes with a little prodding!) That means: going through your home and office Rolodex, PDA or address book; the in-house phone directory from your last company; and the membership list for any organization or association to which you belong.

Your list of initial contacts should have at least a hundred names on it! You can prioritize the names, but you'll be surprised how quickly you get to the "B" and "C" lists. Also keep in mind that it is a growing list. Each name on the list will yield additional names. Don't omit people just because they have no apparent connection with your industry and don't hesitate to tell people that you are looking for a job.

One of the authors personally knows a senior executive who found a job through his gardener and a woman who had obtained several job interviews through her personal shopper at Bergdorf Goodman! Think back – how did *you* get your last job? How about the one before that?

YOUR CONTACTS BASE

- Co-workers and former co-workers
- Clients and former clients
- Suppliers
- Colleagues and competitors
- Family
- Ex-family
- Extended family

- Neighbors/former neighbors
- Classmates and alumni
- Associates from organizations, charities, and religious affiliations
- Acquaintances from a special interest group: health club, sports team, book group, etc.

NETWORKING LETTERS & PHONE CALLS

Once you have been given a referral name, it is up to you to decide whether to call or write the person. In either case, be sure you mention the name of the person who referred you. Unless you have specifically been told that the person you are contacting has a job opening, *approach the person for information.* That means **do not send a resume**. Write a letter that briefly summarizes your experience and outlines the information you are seeking. Do not send an e-mail or a fax unless you are specifically asked to do so.

Before you call the person to whom you have been referred, prepare a script. Know who you are calling, who referred you, and how you would like this person to help you. If you reach a secretary or assistant, give the name of the person who referred you. Sometimes your tone of voice will get you through to the person. If you reach the contact person's voicemail, leave a brief message mentioning the name of the person who referred you and stating the purpose of your call. Be sure to sound positive and professional. SMILE when you leave a message or speak to someone on the phone. (Do it in front of a mirror.) You really can hear a smile! If you don't get a response in 3 to 4 days, call again and leave another message. If you don't hear back and have not written a note in advance, write one now, explaining the reason you are calling. As a last resort, call the person who referred you and ask him to intercede on your behalf.

TELEPHONING CONTACTS

When you call a contact in your industry or in the industry where you would like to work, be sure to make it clear that *you are asking for information* or advice or additional contacts. It is important to make it clear from the beginning that *you are not asking for a job*. A good approach is "I have great respect for your knowledge of the industry and I would like to bounce a few of my ideas off of you."

Remember – *flattery will get you everywhere* when you want help. It is a good idea to keep in mind how you have felt (or would feel) when someone called you to ask for advice or information. Certainly, you didn't feel they were imposing. You were probably flattered. Your calls will be viewed that way, too, if your approach is correct.

It is important to let your contacts know *how they can help you*. Don't expect them to try to figure it out. Ask to be introduced to other people – either specific individuals you would like to meet or people your contact thinks might be informative or helpful. Ask for suggestions of additional companies to target in your search. Ask them for referrals to executive recruiters.

 REMEMBER: You Are Asking For Information, Not A Job!

NETWORKING MEETINGS

Okay, you have persuaded Ms.Warmheart to see you for 15 minutes to give you the benefit of her vast knowledge derived from a 30-year career in the shoe industry.

 KEEP IN MIND:

- This is an informational meeting, not a job interview. Don't walk in and hand her your resume!

- Give a quick synopsis of your background.

- Be specific about the information, advice, or contact names, etc. you would like.

- Honor the time limit you set and extend it only if invited to do so.

- Write a thank-you note to Ms.Warmheart and call or write to follow up with the person who referred you to her.

OTHER WAYS TO NETWORK

- Participate in outside activities.

- Do community service work in an area related to your field of interest.

- Take advantage of your trade association job bank or referral service.

- Contact your college alumni placement service.

IMPLEMENTING YOUR MARKETING PLAN

Now you are ready to implement your personal marketing plan. The next step is to determine what further information you need and how you will use it. Take the time to answer the following questions:

1) What information do I need about target companies and contacts?
2) How will I get the information?
3) Who will be my initial contacts and how will I approach them?
4) What search firms should I contact and how?
5) What publications should I be reading on a regular basis and how will I gain access to them?
6) How will I find out about other companies that I should target?

 REMEMBER:

- Utilize every contact fully and carefully. *The person you least expect could be the one who leads you to your next position.*

- Be open and flexible. Don't prejudge. Pursue all leads even if a company or position doesn't sound like it's for you. Every contact can and should lead to another one.

- Your goal is to have the position offered to you. You can always turn it down. Don't make the company turn you down because you have not shown sufficient interest.

- Research is essential. The more you know about a company, its position in the market place and the key players, the better your presentation will be.

CHAPTER V

RESEARCHING COMPANIES

This section focuses on research sources such as library materials, on-line research vehicles, and a wide variety of industry publications. Devote a day of your job search to familiarizing yourself with the wealth of free information at the public library. Public libraries have subscriptions to on-line services and easy-to-use electronic databases that will provide you with up-to-the-minute information. This section also provides lists of industry-specific resources that you should not overlook.

Research plays an important role at all stages of your job search. It allows you to:

1) Learn more about an organization to prepare for an interview.

2) Delve into the background of an organization or key personnel to evaluate an employment offer.

3) Compile a list of organizations for a target mailing list if networking has been unsuccessful.

4) Develop a list of target organizations to research further.

This section lists standard materials found in most libraries. Libraries have excellent resources including computerized information retrieval, annual reports and business periodicals, all of which should be particularly helpful in your job search. Almost all traditionally printed resources are now also available on-line or in CD-ROM format.

The following are resources and publications that may apply to your search. Your thoroughness and creative thinking will lead you to discover additional research sources.

REFERENCE MATERIALS

FASHION AND TRADE ASSOCIATIONS

American Advertising Federation	www.aaf.org
Advertising Council	www.adcouncil.org
American Association Of Advertising Agencies	www.aaaa.org
American Association Of Exporters And Importers	www.aaei.org
American Textile Manufacturers Institute	www.atmi.org
American Fur Industry	www.nafa.ca
American Apparel & Footwear Association	www.thefashion.org
American Society Of Interior Designers	www.asid.org
Apparel Manufacturers' Association	www.americanapparel.org
Advertising Photographers of America	www.apanational.com
Cosmetics, Toiletries And Fragrance Association	www.ctfa.org
Direct Marketing Association	www.the-dma.org

Council Of Fashion Designers Of America	www.cfda.com
Graphic Artists Guild	www.gag.org
Institute Of Store Planners	www.ispo.org
Jewelry Industry Center	www.jic.org
National Retail Federation	www.nrf.com
Retail Advertising And Marketing Association	www.rama-nrf.com
New York Fashion Designers	www.fashionwindows.com
RSVP Directory	www.rsvpdirectory.com
Fashion Group International	www.fgi.org
The Woolmark Company	www.wool.com
Fur Information Council of America	www.fur.org
Yarn Textile Associations	www.unitedyarn.com

DIRECTORIES

Directory of Corporate Affiliations	www.corporateaffiliations.com
Directory of Executive Recruiters	www.kennedyinfo.com
Directory of Management Consultants	www.kennedyinfo.com
Dun & Bradstreet Reference Books	www.dnb.com
Directory of Associations	www.marketingsource.com
Franchises	www.franchise.com
Harris Industrial Directory	www.harrisinfo.com
International Directory of Corporate Affiliations	www.corporateaffiliations.com
Manufacturers Directory	www.thomasregional.com
Places Rated Almanac	www.wiley.com
Reference Book of Corporate Management	www.hoovers.com
Standard & Poors	www.standardandpoors.com
Ward's Business Directory	www.galegroup.com

NEWSPAPERS

The Wall Street Journal	www.wsj.com
The New York Times	www.nytimes.com
National Business Employment Weekly	www.epinions.com
Crain's New York Business	www.crainsny.com
The National Ad Search	www.nationaladsearch.com

MAGAZINES

Business Week	www.businessweek.com
Forbes	www.forbes.com
Fortune	www.fortune.com

INDUSTRY SPECIFIC REFERENCE MATERIALS

Davison's Textile Bluebook	www.davisonbluebook.com
O'Dwyer's Public Relations Directory	www.odwyerpr.com
The Salesman's Guide	www.salesmansguide.com
Thomas' Register of American Manufacturers	www.thomasregister.com

The next five can all be found at www.fairchildpub.com
WWD Buyer's Guides
WWD Supplier's Guide
WWD/DNR The Business Newsletter for Specialty Stores
Fairchild's Textile Directory
Fairchild's Retail Directory

TRADE PERIODICALS

ADVERTISING INDUSTRY

Ad Week	www.adweek.com
Advertising Age	www.adage.com
DM News	www.dmnews.com
Catalog Age	www.catalogmag.com
Direct Marketing	www.dmnews.com

BEAUTY INDUSTRY

Beauty Fashion	www. beautyfashion.com
Cosmetic World	www.cosmeticworld.com
WWD Beauty Biz	www.fairchildpub.com

TOY INDUSTRY

The Toy Book	www.adventurepub.com
Playthings	www.playthings.com
Knitting Times	www.asktmag.com
Children's Business	www.childrensbusiness.com

SALES AND MARKETING

The Competitive Advantage	www.competitiveadvatage.com
The Bottom Line-Personal	
Boardroom Reports	www.boardroom.com

VISUAL DISPLAY AND PACKAGING

VM&SD	www.stpubs.com
How Magazine	www.usubscribe.com
POP Times	www.popshow.com
International Design	www.idonline.com
Graphis	www.graphis.com
Packaging	www.packworld.com
Packaging Monthly	www.mindbranch.com

INTIMATE APPAREL

BF/IA	www.bfia.com

CHILDREN'S WEAR

Children's Business	www.childrensbusiness.com
Earnshaw's	

HOME FASHIONS

LDB	www.interiortextiles.com
Floor Covering Weekly	www.floorcoveringweekly.com
HFN	www.fairchildpub.com
Home Accents Today	www.homeaccentstoday.com
Home Textiles Today	www.hometextilestoday.com
Tableware Today	www.tablewaretoday.com

GENERAL APPAREL AND TEXTILE

AAMA Newsletter	www.americanapparel.org
Apparel Industry Magazine	www.aimagazine.com
Apparel News Group	www.apparelnews.net
Bobbin	www.bobbin.com
Daily News Record	www.dnrnews.com
Fiberarts	www.fiberartsmagazine.com
Textile Industries	www.textileindustries.com
Textile World	www.textileworld.com
Women's Wear Daily	www.wwd.com

ACCESSORIES

Accessories Magazine	www.amagazinearea.com
Accessory Merchandising	www.vancepublications.com
American Jewelry Manufacturer	www.ajm-magazine.com
Footwear News	www.footwearnews.com
Jewelers' Circular Keystone	www.jckgroup.com
Metalsmith	www.snagmetalsmith.org

Advertiser & Agency Red Book Plus	www.redbooks.com
National Trade Data Bank	www.stat-usa.gov
NEXIS	www.nexis.com
Textile Technology Digest	www.itt.edu/ttdd
Thomas' Register	www.thomasregister.com

ON-LINE AND INTERNET RESEARCH

CAREER & JOB SEARCH WEB SITES

Websites often change the location of pages so if a page is no longer available, check the home page of the website for an updated link.

Fashion Career Websites
www.24sevenonline.com/candidate/welcome.asp
http:fashion.about.com/cs/jobboards
www.ApparelSearch.com
www.fashion-career.com
www.fashioncareercenter.com
www.jobfactory.com/indus/indus122.htm
www.retail-recruiter.com
www.stylecareers.com

Fashion Industry Resources
www.fashioncenter.com
www.infomat.com

General Career Websites
www.hotjobs.yahoo.com
www.nytimes.com/pages/jobs/index.html
www.careerbuilder.com
www.careermag.com
www.careeronestop.org
www.collegegrad.com
www.flipdog.com
www.jobbankusa.com
www.jobfind.com
www.jobtrack.com
www.jobweb.org
www.latimes.com/classified/jobs/?track=lajobslefttop
www.monster.com
www.nationjob.com

Career Website Portals
www.astec-inc.com
www.hotbot.com/default.asp?prov=Google&tab=web&query=careers
www.usnews.com/usnews/work/wohome.htm

NOTES:

CHAPTER VI

THE INTERVIEW

TYPES OF INTERVIEWS

There are essentially two types of interviews: the Networking or Informational Interview and the Employment Interview. Whether you are networking or interviewing for a specific position, *you must know your objective or purpose in meeting with the interviewer*. You want to tell your story, to obtain leads, to explore a particular job opportunity, etc. Knowing the purpose will help you focus and make the best use of the time allotted to you.

Interviewing can be very stressful. It is possible to alleviate some of that stress by examining specific aspects of the interview process. Start by thinking of the interview as a sales presentation. The product you are selling is yourself, your skills and your experience. As with any sales presentation, the keys are *practice and preparation*!

Networking Interviews, which we discussed in Chapter IV, are typically informal meetings with people you know or to whom you have been personally referred. The purpose of these meetings is to gain information and ideas about:

- An industry
- A company
- Executive recruiters
- Potential employers
- Specific job opportunities
- Referrals to further contacts in the industry

 REMEMBER:

Before or during these meetings, you must make it clear that you are *not* asking the person for a job. You should come prepared with a list of the questions you want to ask rather than your resume. If the person asks for a resume, offer to mail one to him and do so with your *thank-you note*!

Employment Interviews, which we will concentrate on in this section, are those that involve *specific* job opportunities.

EMPLOYMENT INTERVIEWS

STAGES OF THE INTERVIEW

1) **Opening:** This includes shaking hands firmly and being offered a chair. A skilled interviewer will attempt to break the ice and make the interviewee relax and feel at ease.

2) **Down to Business – Discussion & Questions:** The interviewer may briefly discuss the job and company or organization. Listen carefully and think about how you can fit in and help them.

3) **Closing:** Sensing when an interview is ending will become easier with practice. Be sure to discuss what the next step will be before you leave and SMILE when you say goodbye.

Salary is not usually discussed until the interviewer has determined that you are a viable candidate. This rarely happens in an initial interview.

INTERACTION WITH THE INTERVIEWER – IMPORTANT POINTS TO BEAR IN MIND

Connections – This is an opportunity to make a personal connection with the interviewer. Be sensitive to what he/she picks up on and expand upon it.

Highlight Attributes – Be sure to bring out accomplishments or personal characteristics wherever possible. If you can, try to relate them to the specific job for which you are interviewing.

Adapt to your Audience – If the interviewer is familiar with your business, it is okay to mention specific company names, technical terms or jargon of that industry. If the person does not know the business, don't try to dazzle him with names or terminology that are meaningless to him. It may make you sound pretentious, not knowledgeable!

Be Aware of the Listener – If the interviewer does not interrupt, watch his body language carefully. Are his eyes glazing over? Is he looking at his watch? Try to gauge whether he is interested or tuning you out. Brevity is crucial. Do not get carried away with your own story.

 NOTE: *There are many different types of interviewing styles. Be prepared for anything!*

YOUR RESPONSIBILITIES:

Be well prepared – Research the company!

Be properly dressed – Look professional!

Be alert, interested and enthusiastic – Maintain eye contact. Don't slouch!

Adapt to the interviewer's style.

Answer the questions posed – Don't volunteer information unless it is relevant. Hear the questions and answer them.

LISTEN!!! This is the key to a successful interview. *Not listening is the most common mistake people make.*

Ask insightful questions – The interview is a two-way street. While the interviewer is determining how you will fit, you are finding out about the culture of the company, the position, the department and how you would fit in from your perspective!

Ask for clarification. If a question is unclear, don't try to guess what the person means.

 REMEMBER:

- Be sure the interviewer knows what you want him/her to know about you. Many interviewers like to talk. If you have not had a chance to cover areas you feel are important, say *"Before we close, there are a couple of things I'd like you to know about me...."*

- Ask what the next step is (When and with whom is your next meeting?) Inquire about follow-up timing. (When should you expect to hear from them or should you call them?)

- Express your interest and desire to continue the process. (Don't assume they know your feelings.)

- Always ask for a business card. This will help you manage your search so that you will have the exact name, title and address of the person for follow-up and your thank-you note*!*

THE 3-MINUTE INTRODUCTION
(The Professionals' Secret to Successful Interviewing)

Professional outplacement and career counselors often teach their clients this technique, which serves a multitude of purposes in the job search. It can be used for networking calls and meetings and, most importantly, it is the response to that frequently asked interview question: *"Tell me about yourself."*

Once you have mastered this technique you will approach the interview with more confidence, knowing that you can verbalize your strengths and accomplishments and have the ability to set the tone for the meeting.

The general idea is to *briefly* communicate your recent experience and accomplishments to the interviewer and give a picture of yourself as a complete person; someone with whom he or she would enjoy working.

The basic outline for this presentation is as follows:

PART I – CURRENT OR MOST RECENT POSITION
- Job Title/Description
- 1 or 2 Accomplishments
- If appropriate, you may want to discuss your progression in the organization or increased responsibilities and mention a few more accomplishments. Use your judgment.

PART II – EARLY LIFE & EDUCATION
- Place of birth
- Any unusual or interesting aspects of your early life regarding yourself or your family or activities of note — scholastic, sports, extra-curricular
- College degrees/activities

PART III – CAREER PATH
- First job or how you started in the business you are in. Mention military experience here, if applicable.
- Key job moves or promotions. Work forward chronologically to current company and position in Part I.
- Career changes if any and how they came about.
- Work-related courses or training; travel etc. (It is not necessary to include all of these. Keep it brief and interesting!)

PART IV – CLOSE AND TRANSFER
- Mention reason for leaving and/or why you are there.
- Steer the conversation back to the interviewer by saying something to the effect of: *"I would like to learn more about your company and I am sure that you have many more questions for me...."*

PREPARING THE 3-MINUTE INTRODUCTION

Begin by writing out this introduction in complete sentences in the chronology outlined on the previous page. Then read it aloud and time yourself. Then edit it to 2 to 3 minutes. Then *PRACTICE, PRACTICE, PRACTICE!!!*

With your presentation "in memory" you can select portions to suit different situations:

- A quick overview for contacts, to refresh their memory
- A 1-2 minute summary in a telephone interview

When it comes time to put the full presentation to use, you will want to be as *natural* and *enthusiastic* as possible. You can do this by practicing your presentation aloud, not memorizing it. Tailor the presentation to your audience. Make *eye contact* with the listener and adapt to his or her responses. *Be flexible* – you may not get through the entire story uninterrupted. The interviewer will almost always pick up on something you say or ask a question. Don't worry about adhering to your presentation. The purpose is to engage the interviewer. Remember – this should not sound rehearsed!

THE REASON-FOR-LEAVING STATEMENT

The purpose of the Reason-for-Leaving Statement is to be able to give a positive, truthful, comfortable and brief answer to the question "why did you leave your last position?"

Draft and edit your statement until you are satisfied with it. This process will keep your reason for leaving concise and help ensure that you have it firmly in your mind. Review it with your ex-employers and get their agreement so that you and your former organization will communicate with a consistent message.

 NOTE – When You Draft Your Statement:

- **Keep it short.** Generally, the more you try to explain, the more difficult it gets. You will be prepared to answer follow-up questions, but only if they are asked.

- **Be as positive as possible.** Negative statements about your former boss or company will only hurt you.

- **Put your best foot forward but be truthful.** There are a number of factors that result in a person's leaving. Pick the one that is most positive and easiest to explain.

Review the sample reason-for-leaving statements on the next page. Then, with these thoughts in mind, try your hand at drafting your reason-for-leaving statement.

SAMPLE REASON-FOR-LEAVING STATEMENTS

New Boss

"I have had many rewarding years at an outstanding company and I have contributed to a number of successes in the division. About 2 years ago my boss retired. It has become apparent that my new manager and I have different management styles and methods of operating. I became convinced that it would be easier to attain my career goals outside the company."

Restructuring/Downsizing to Eliminate Job

"Like many businesses in the industry, my company is going through a major restructuring and downsizing. Unfortunately, this has meant the elimination of several management positions, including my own. I am disappointed, of course, because I am proud of the contributions I have made to the company. But I also consider this an opportunity to put my skills and experience to work in a new setting."

Reorganization/Changed Responsibilities

"I have worked with this company for many years and have learned a great deal as I progressed through store operations, buying and divisional merchandising positions. The recent corporate shift to "matrix" management, however has lifted many responsibilities I previously held to higher levels within the organization. As this has reduced my opportunities to grow personally and professionally, I am seeking new opportunities outside the company."

Buyout/Early Retirement Offer

"My many years at this company have been challenging and rewarding. I was fortunate to have held several positions in which I contributed significantly to improving the company's bottom line. Recently, senior management made a major shift in our product line. Several of us were offered a choice between accepting a new role in the corporate structure and taking a voluntary buyout. Quite frankly, I thought the buyout was just too good a financial package to pass up. And I feel confident that my experience as a results-oriented executive will be valuable to a new employer."

Closing Own Business

"Although I have enjoyed many aspects of being in my own business and have learned a great deal, I miss the interchange of ideas and the stimulation of working with other people in a team environment."

Or

"My management style has always been very hands-on. As a consultant, I have felt removed from the daily work environment. I would like to return to a situation where I can participate in the implementation of ideas and see projects through to fruition."

QUESTIONS TO ASK IN AN INTERVIEW

You will want to ask questions that will help you determine if the position is "a fit" for your skills, interests and career goals. These questions should also serve to communicate to the interviewer your interest and enthusiasm, as well as the fact that you have done your homework about the company.

SUGGESTED QUESTIONS:

1) Tell me about the nature of the position. What are the specific responsibilities? Is a written job description available?

2) To whom does the position report? Can you tell me something about his/her background?

3) Who are the key people in other departments with whom I would interface?

4) Is this a newly created position? If not, who was the last person to hold the position and what are they doing now?

5) What type of training can I expect in the first six months? Down the road?

6) What would be the opportunities for advancement within the organization?

7) What are the travel requirements, if any?

8) What is the structure of the department? Is it fully staffed or would I be expected to hire a staff?

DIFFICULT QUESTIONS INTERVIEWERS ASK

Below are common interview questions for which *you should have answers prepared*. It is a good idea to write out the answers to all of these questions; then read and refine those answers so you are PREPARED.

1) Tell me about yourself. (See "The 3-Minute Introduction" section on page 64.)

2) Where do you see yourself five years from now? Ten years?

3) What are your strengths/weaknesses?

4) Tell me about the worst boss you have ever had.

5) What is your current salary?

6) What is your management style?

7) Why should we hire you?

8) What do you think you could offer (contribute to) this company?

9) If you could start again, what would you do differently?

10) How do you rate yourself as an executive?

11) What features of your previous jobs have you disliked?

12) Why do you think you would like to work for this company?

13) Give some examples of situations in which your work was criticized.

14) What is the most difficult work situation you encountered and how did you handle it?

15) If we were to call your last employer, what would he/she say about you?

16) How do you handle stress?

17) Why do you want to leave (did you leave) your last position? (See the Reason-for-Leaving Statement on page 65)

There are no right answers to these questions. Every case is an individual one and the answers you give will depend on your own situation and objectives. Just be positive. Don't dwell on negative experiences.

It is particularly important to prepare answers to the questions "Tell me about yourself" and "Why did you leave your last position?" The preceding techniques will help you develop those answers.

SAMPLE LETTERS

THE COVER LETTER FOR YOUR RESUME

A resume needs a covering letter to personalize it and to request an interview. In other words, good cover letter writing must take into consideration that the end result you seek is employer action. More specifically, you want the recipient to grant you an interview.

Before composing a letter, research the company and position. (See Chapter V of this manual for a listing of reference sources.) Extensive information can be found on the Internet or in the public library. Be sure to familiarize yourself with the company's product line or service and try to ascertain its problems.

Your cover letter should not be longer than three or four paragraphs and should never exceed one page. Remember that most in your audience are very busy and are inundated with reading material, especially correspondence. In addition to specific resume cover letters, you will need the following:

1) **Ad response cover letters** to accompany your resume in answer to newspaper or professional journal advertisements.
2) **Internet cover letters** required by some web sites – essentially a summary of your qualifications
3) **Search firm letters** to accompany your resume.
4) **Target company letters** that you can send to decision makers in organizations where you do not have a contact. Target company letters do not include a resume.
5) **Interview follow-up and thank-you letters.** It is perfectly acceptable to hand write these if your handwriting is legible.

Most of your letters will cover the following points:
- The purpose for letter: to respond to an ad, to introduce yourself to a search firm, to help the company solve a problem.
- Your professional background: career highlights and key accomplishments.
- Your personal attributes: the characteristics, insights, personality traits that make you distinctive.
- And the next step: *take the initiative* for follow-up communications.

On the following pages you will find some sample letters of the various types mentioned above.

COVER LETTER FORMAT

LETTERHEAD
June 15, 2003
Ms. Jane Jones
Title
Company
Street Address
City, State, Zip Code

Dear Ms. Jones:

FIRST PARAGRAPH:

Explain why you are writing; name the position for which you are applying. Explain how you heard of the opening.

SECOND PARAGRAPH:

Use this paragraph to highlight qualifications you present in your resume that would be of greatest interest to the employer. Explain why you are particularly interested in this company and type of work. If you have had related experience, or specialized training, be sure to point it out.

THIRD PARAGRAPH:

Close by making a specific request for an interview. Make sure your closing is not vague, and makes reference to specific action from the reader. If possible, leave control for the next step in your own hands, suggesting you will follow up with a telephone call.

Sincerely yours,

(Your hand-written signature)

Type your name

AD RESPONSE LETTER
(Hiring company and recruiter identified)

WILLIAM WORKMAN
400 Duane Street
New York, NY 10009
(212) 896-4596
willwork@yourcompany.com

June 15, 2003

Ms. Joan M. Igotajob
Vice President, Human Resources
J.C. Penney Co., Inc.
P.O. Box 659000
Dallas, TX 75265

Dear Ms. Igotajob:

Your recent advertisement in Women's Wear Daily for an Advertising Vice-President outlines skills and experience that are an excellent match to my background.

As Advertising Director for Macy's Northeast, with a budget of $20 million, I accomplished several objectives highlighted in your ad:

- Developed successful Father's Day television campaign, resulting in 20% increase in same store sales for men's furnishings.

- Screened and selected new outside agency for direct mail and billboard/bus stop advertising.

- Negotiated new media contract with local cable TV station resulting in $500,000 savings over 2 years.

I have a Bachelor's Degree in Journalism from Columbia University, supplemented by experience in both the editorial and advertising areas of fashion publishing. My background also encompasses extensive retail advertising experience on the client side.

Enclosed is my resume for your review. I am confident that my proven ability in print as well as electronic media advertising would be valuable to J.C. Penney as you continue to meet the challenges of this new age in advertising. In addition to my home number listed above, I can be reached during business hours at (212) 256-4217 to further discuss my background.

Sincerely,

William Workman

Enclosure (resume)

AD RESPONSE LETTER
(Blind ad, salary information requested)

WILLIAM WORKMAN
401 Duane Street
New York, NY 10009
(212) 896-4596
willwork@yourcompany.com

June 15, 2003

Box 29
New York Times
New York, New York 06122

Dear Sir/Madam:

Enclosed is my resume in response to your recent advertisement for a Marketing Director. It outlines fifteen years of consumer products marketing experience and skills that match the requirements your ad describes.

Of particular note is my expertise in brand management. I am especially proud of having created the successful "Captivating" fragrance image campaign as well as the "Loveliness" skincare line introduction.

During my career, I have also enjoyed and been commended for my ability to develop and execute innovative strategies to reduce the initial costs of a product introduction without negatively impacting the result.

My academic credentials include an M.B.A. in Marketing from the University of Chicago. My current compensation is in the low six figures, but my focus is on finding an opportunity where I can utilize my skills and experience in a challenging environment.

I look forward to an opportunity to discuss my background in a personal interview. In addition to my home number above, I can be reached during business hours at (818) 322-1172.

Sincerely,

William Workman

Enclosure (resume)

INTERNET COVER LETTER
(Response to a specific job listing requesting cover letter and resume)

WILLIAM WORKMAN
402 Duane Street
New York, NY 10009
(212) 896-4596
willwork@yourcompany.com

June 15, 2003

ABC Corporation
1234 Beachwood Street
Cleveland, Ohio 30322

Dear Sir/Madam:

Your job description for a Vice President of Sales seeks experience that closely parallels my own. I am an experienced sales executive with a track record of consistent volume increases in the moderate sportswear market. I have strong managerial and administrative skills as well as proven ability to lead and motivate a sales team. Below are some highlights of my career:

MANAGEMENT
- Built strong sales teams and support staff
- Converted independent road force to an in-house sales staff, increasing profitability by 12%
- Organized all aspects of sales operations for $60 million division

SALES
- Turned 28% sales decline into a 39% increase in 2 years
- Introduced 3 new product lines

PRESENTATIONS
- Developed and presented sales education seminars for retail associates
- Conducted presentations of new product lines to retail management
- Created Power Point presentations of boutique proposals for retail executives

NEGOTIATING SKILLS
- Successfully negotiated increased space allotments
- Created strong retail partnerships
- Negotiated increased advertising and direct mail space

I am confident that I can make a significant contribution to the growth of your existing business and the introduction of new lines. I look forward to having the opportunity to further discuss my qualifications with you.

Sincerely,

Will Workman

CONTINGENCY SEARCH FIRM LETTER

WILLIAM WORKMAN
403 Duane Street
New York, NY 10009
(212) 896-4596
willwork@yourcompany.com

June 15, 2003

Mr. John Willhelp
Executive Search Consultants, Inc.
1061 E. 15th St.
Chicago, IL 20266

Dear Mr. Willhelp:

As you search for experienced manufacturing professionals, please consider my credentials:

- More than 15 years experience in production control, scheduling and planning with two of the largest companies in the fashion accessories industry.

- Recognized expertise in negotiating with suppliers of raw materials and findings.

- Proven ability to work with merchandising and sales to produce a quality product at a reasonable cost.

I would like to put this expertise to work in a senior production position for a medium to large manufacturer. My compensation, currently in the high $80s, is only one of many factors that I will use to evaluate opportunities.

I look forward to hearing from you and would welcome the opportunity to discuss my background in more detail. To avoid duplicating our efforts, please call me before forwarding my resume to any of your clients.

Sincerely,

William Workman

Enclosure (resume)

TARGET COMPANY LETTER

WILLIAM WORKMAN
404 Duane Street
New York, NY 10009
(212) 896-4596
willwork@yourcompany.com

June 15, 2003

Mr. Kim Job
EVP, Chief Administrative Officer
Kmart Corporation
3100 West Big Beaver Road
Troy, MI 48004

Dear Mr. Job:

Recent studies indicate that by the year 2000, companies will be competing for a shortage of highly skilled employees. Successful companies will be those that do a first rate job of selecting, training, and, most importantly, developing their employees. Twenty years of experience specializing in *organizational development*, *performance improvement*, and *human resource planning* gives me a unique opportunity to help Kmart meet that challenge.

During my career, I have designed, implemented, and evaluated a wide variety of organization development interventions. Of particular interest are my experiences in establishing and operating assessment centers for improved employee selection and training as well as the design and implementation of quality circle and employee involvement efforts.

This hands-on experience has been supplemented by intensive academic training: a Ph.D. in Human and Organization Systems and a M.S. in Management, concentrating on Organization Behavior and Industrial Relations. The latter degree was earned at Northwestern University, where I also received my undergraduate degree.

In this brief synopsis, I have tried to highlight my background, but would welcome the opportunity to discuss these issues in more detail. I will call you next week to explore how these skills might be utilized in the Kmart organization.

Sincerely,

William Workman

RETAINER SEARCH FIRM LETTER

WILLIAM WORKMAN
405 Duane Street
New York, NY 10009
(212) 896-4596
willwork@yourcompany.com

June 15, 2003

Ms. Gay Young
Lord Associates, Inc.
456 Madison Ave.
New York, NY l0023

Dear Ms. Young:

If you have a client seeking a highly motivated manager with a demonstrated record of success, please consider the following credentials:

- Ten years of general management responsibility, most recently as Vice President and General Manager of an international operation with $90 million in annual sales.

- Four years experience in international operations.

- Proven record of turning around troubled divisions.

- Academic credentials, which include an MBA with an emphasis in Industrial Relations and a B.B.A in Accounting.

I seek a general management position with full profit and loss responsibility. While I have an extensive background in the intimate apparel industry, the skills and knowledge I have acquired are applicable to many fields of business. My recent base compensation has been in the low $80's, with additional executive incentives. At 49, with two grown children, my wife and I are free to relocate.

My resume is enclosed for your review. I would welcome the opportunity to discuss it in more detail and will call you next week to arrange an appointment.

Sincerely,

William Workman

Enclosure (resume)

SAMPLE FOLLOW-UP THANK-YOU LETTER
EXECUTIVE RECRUITER
(Now employed)

WILLIAM WORKMAN
406 Duane Street
New York, NY 10009
(212) 896-4596
willwork@yourcompany.com

June 15, 2003

Ms. Jane Doe
Principal
Helpful Associates, Inc.
425 Lexington Avenue
New York, NY 10027

Dear Ms. Doe:

I wanted to let you know that I have accepted the position of Store Manager of World Wide Industries in Reading, Pennsylvania, a $3.5 billion retailer of interior furnishings. I will be in charge of the company's largest store, at 30,000 sq. ft., with a staff of 250 and annual sales of over $60 million.

As you may recall, I was previously Store Manager of Bombay Industries Co. in Dallas, Texas.

I appreciated your support during my search. If I can be of assistance in providing referrals for your future searches, please do not hesitate to call me at (717) 391-1234.

With best wishes,

William Workman

THANK YOU LETTER
(Follow up to employment interview)

WILLIAM WORKMAN
407 Duane Street
New York, NY 10009
(212) 896-4596
willwork@yourcompany.com

June 15, 2003

Mr. Sam Leigh
President
The Brown Company
345 Fifth Avenue
New York, NY 123265

Dear Mr. Leigh:

I enjoyed meeting with you on Monday to discuss my interest in your Knitwear Designer position.

Pursuant to our conversation, I would like to tell you a bit more about my relevant experience. Working directly with the Director of Merchandising, I have conceptualized and designed three successful knitwear lines, graphed patterns, speced garments, and selected colors and yarns. Additionally, I managed the technical design aspects of the production process, both domestically and overseas.

I am enthusiastic about the new direction you are planning for the line and feel that my skills and background make me particularly well-qualified to develop and execute the concept. As you suggested, I will call you next week to follow-up on our interview.

Sincerely,

William Workman

CHAPTER VIII

THE JOB OFFER

When an offer is extended, you have reached a significant milestone in the search process. Whether or not you feel it is the right job for you, knowing that an offer is extended is a great boost psychologically. It also increases your leverage to attract other offers.

CRITERIA TO CONSIDER

YOUR PERSONAL GOALS

Y N

☐ ☐ Are your basic job objective criteria met?

☐ ☐ Does this position meet your goals?

☐ ☐ Will you be doing what you like to do and are good at?

☐ ☐ Will you be challenged?

☐ ☐ Are your inner feelings positive or negative?

THE COMPANY CULTURE

Y N

☐ ☐ Are you comfortable with the company culture? Atmosphere?

☐ ☐ Is the company well positioned in its market for short/long term growth?

☐ ☐ Do your skills, interests and values match the functions of the job and the company culture?

☐ ☐ Is there potential for advancement and career growth?

THE COMPANY STRUCTURE

Y N

☐ ☐ Do you feel you understand the hierarchy?

☐ ☐ Do you understand what the decision-making process is?

☐ ☐ Have you met your boss's boss?

☐ ☐ Are the reporting relationships clear or is there ambiguity?

☐ ☐ Do you think you understand what your supervisors would expect of you?

☐ ☐ Are the resources on hand for you to get the job done?

☐ ☐ Are the rewards and potential there?

☐ ☐ Are performance reviews fixed? How are rewards made for good performers?

EXAMINING THE FINANCIAL ASPECTS OF THE OFFER

Obviously the financial aspects are as important to consider as the position itself. Both are interrelated, but each should be considered independently.

The value of benefits today may be as important as the salary and incentives. Analyze the whole compensation package with a trusted friend or advisor. In some cases, it may be helpful to consult a lawyer and/or an accountant for assistance in evaluating the pros and cons. You should have maximum input to aid you in your decision.

Take into consideration not only the salary, but also the entire compensation package that could include any of the following perks and benefits:

base salary
bonus
profit sharing
sales commissions
expense accounts
medical insurance
dental insurance
life insurance
spouse life insurance
long-term care insurance
death benefit payment
insurance benefits after termination
vacations, free travel
company car or gas allowance
stock options
matching investment program
country club membership
annual physical exam
luncheon club membership
athletic club membership
disability pay
pension plan/401K program
legal assistance

executive dining room privileges
financial planning assistance
overseas travel, spouse travel
C.P.A. and tax assistance
moving expenses
mortgage rate differential
mortgage prepayment penalty
real estate brokerage
closing costs
bridge loan
trips for your family to look for a home
lodging fees while between homes
shipping of boats and pets
installation of appliances, carpeting, etc.
mortgage funds
short-term loans
company purchase of your home
deferred compensation
consumer product discounts
severance pay
consulting fees after termination
outplacement

SALARY NEGOTIATIONS

- Most employers will not try to exploit you. Approach the negotiations with trust and goodwill.

- The employer's job: to hire you at the lowest reasonable salary.

- Your job: to be hired at the highest reasonable salary.

- The difference between #2 and #3 is the negotiable area. It can be as much as 20%, (about $8,000 at the $40,000 level.)

- Fringe benefits are worth 25%, and more, of the base salary. If the benefits are lower, the salary should be proportionately higher.

- It is important to keep in mind that the salary offer may be determined to some extent on your previous salary. Many companies are reluctant to offer more than a 10% to 15% increase over your last job. You may be asked to produce a W-2 from the previous year so don't exaggerate the salary. Focus on your previous total compensation package instead.

It's a tough market out there. Don't sell yourself short, but if you really feel good about the job, a few thousand dollars in salary may not be worth haggling over.

ACCEPTANCE AND CONFIRMATION

While you are considering your initial offer, *you should continue to pursue other opportunities.* Do not feel that you have to give a prospective employer an immediate response. It is reasonable to expect to be given enough time to thoroughly evaluate the offer.

When your decision is made and communicated to your new employer, it is important that the offer be *confirmed in writing.* In the case of a company that is not accustomed to doing this as a matter of course, ask for a letter stating your job title and outlining the base salary, all benefits and perks and the agreed-upon starting date. In some instances, you may need to write the letter yourself and ask to have it signed by the appropriate person in the company.

Do not notify anyone of your new position until the confirmation letter has been finalized.

CLOSING OUT YOUR SEARCH

Whether you start your new job immediately or in a few days or weeks, there are some key steps that you must take to bring your search to a close. These are:

- Notify any prospective companies where interviews are scheduled, indicating your decision.

- Write follow-up thank-you letters to all key references, contacts and interested parties who aided in your search and advise them of your decision.

- Review your planning calendar to make sure that all commitments are fulfilled.

- Keep the paperwork you have generated during your search, including all addresses and phone numbers so that you will have it for reference the next time!

Good luck!

About the Authors

 BETH PHILLIPS is the President of Phillips International, which was established in 1984. The company advises its international clients on a complete range of business services including import/export marketing and sales, business management and cross-cultural communications. Ms. Phillips has traveled worldwide to identify producers of high quality fashion and home fashion products committed to building successful international markets.

Beth Phillips is also a faculty member in the College of Media Arts and Design at Drexel University in Philadelphia, where she develops and teaches courses in product development, international retailing, business planning and career development.

 WENDY B. SAMUEL spent over 20 years in the fashion industry, first as a sales representative for high fashion European designers and later, as an executive search consultant for fashion manufacturers and retailers. She has counseled fashion industry executives on career and job searches throughout her career. Ms Samuel is currently a Professional Organizer creating organization out of chaos for home and small businesses under the auspices of Clutter Therapy.

 RENEE PALMER is a former fashion industry executive who held marketing and product development positions at luxury goods companies such as Christian Dior, Coach Leatherware, Mark Cross and Hermès. In a major career change, Ms Palmer began focusing her interests on the electronic commerce channel and joined IBM as an Interactive Marketing Strategist. Ms Palmer is currently a multimedia web strategist for Pink Rat, LLC.

ACKNOWLEDGMENTS

Cover Design by Shari Saffioti - she did what no one else could.

A special thank you to Lee Matzkin for her contribution to the new edition.

Many thanks to Barbara McDonald, Patricia Steele and Joan Watkins for their friendship, love and support.